GREAT PIANO ADAGIOS

60 Works from Bach to Debussy

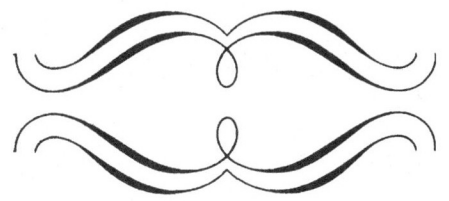

Edited by
DAVID DUTKANICZ

DOVER PUBLICATIONS, INC.
Mineola, New York

Copyright

Copyright © 2005 by Dover Publications, Inc.
All rights reserved.

Bibliographical Note

Great Piano Adagios, first published in 2005, is a new compilation of works reproduced from early authoritative editions.

International Standard Book Number
ISBN-13: 978-0-486-44630-1
ISBN-10: 0-486-44630-1

Manufactured in the United States by LSC Communications
44630105   2018
www.doverpublications.com

Great Piano Adagios
60 Works from Bach to Debussy

BACH, J.S
Prelude in C Major	2
Sinfonia in F Minor	4
Aria	6

SCARLATTI, D.
Sonata in D Minor	7

HANDEL, G.F.
Largo	8
Sarabande in D Minor	10

HAYDN, J.
Sonata No. 6, 3rd mvt.	11
Sonata No. 24, 3rd mvt.	14
Sonata No. 29, 3rd mvt.	17

MOZART, W.A.
Sonata No. 12, 3rd mvt.	20
Sonata No. 14, 3rd mvt.	23
Sonata No. 18, 2nd mvt.	27

BEETHOVEN, L. van
Sonata No. 8, "Pathetique", 2nd mvt.	30
Sonata No. 14, "Moonlight", 1st mvt.	34
Für Elise	38

CHOPIN, F.
Nocturne, Op. 37, No. 1	42
Prelude, Op. 28, No. 4	46
Prelude, Op. 28, No. 6	47
Prelude, Op. 28, No. 20	48

LISZT, F.
Consolation No. 3	49
Consolation No. 4	52

MENDELSSOHN, F.
Sonata in G Minor, Op. 105, 2nd mvt.	53
SONGS WITHOUT WORDS	
Adagio *from* Op. 30, No. 3	56
Adagio *from* Op. 53, No. 4	57

SCHUBERT, F.
Adagio in E Major	58
Adagio *from* Adagio and Rondo, Op. 145	62

SCHUBERT-LISZT
Der Doppelgänger	63

SCHUMANN, ROBERT
Traumerei	68
Child Falling Asleep	69
Warum?	70
Eusebius	71
Abendlied	72

SCHUMANN, CLARA
Larghetto	73

BRAHMS, J.
Intermezzo in E-flat Minor	75

FIELD, J.
Nocturne No. 9	79
Nocturne No. 14	81
Nocturne No. 15	83

DVOŘÁK, A.
On the Holy Mountain	85

JANÁČEK, L.
In Tears	88

TCHAIKOVSKY, P.I.
Song of the Lark	90
The Sick Doll	92
Doll's Burial	93
Morning Prayer	94

BORODIN, A.
In the Convent	95

MOUSSORGSKY, M.
A Tear	98
Catacombs-Roman Sepulchre	100

CUI, C.
Prelude in A-flat Major	102

ALKAN, C.V.
The Dying	105

FRANCK, C.
Slow Dance	108

MASSANET, J.
Élégie	110

SCRIABIN, A.
Prelude, Op. 74, No. 4	112
Prelude, Op. 16, No. 4	114

SAINT-SAËNS, C.
The Swan	115

ARENSKY, A.
Elegy in G Minor	118

MACDOWELL, E.
WOODLAND SKETCHES	
To A Wild Rose	122
Deserted Farm	124

GRIEG, E.
Morning Mood	126

DEBUSSY, C.
Girl with the Flaxen Hair	131
Claire de Lune	133
Jimbo's Lullaby	139

Prelude in C Major
from *The Well-Tempered Clavier I*, BWV 846

Johann Sebastian Bach

Sinfonia in F Minor
from *Three-Part Inventions,* BWV 795

Johann Sebastian Bach

5

Aria
from *Goldberg Variations*, BWV 988

Johann Sebastian Bach

Sonata in D Minor
K34/L S7/P15

Domenico Scarlatti

Largo
from *Xerxes*

George Frideric Handel

9

Sarabande in D Minor
from *Suite in D Minor*

George Frideric Handel

Sonata No. 6
3rd Movement

Joseph Haydn

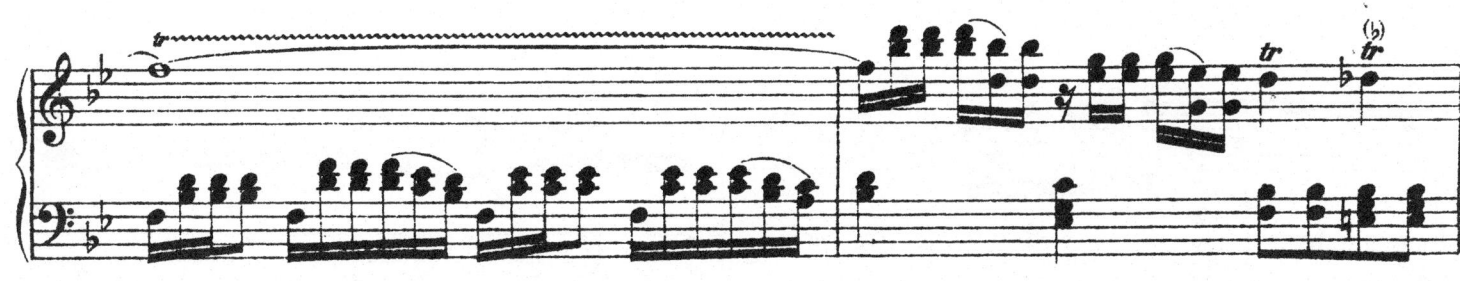

Sonata No. 24
3rd Movement

Joseph Haydn

Sonata No. 29
3rd Movement

Joseph Haydn

Sonata No. 12
K.332, 3rd Movement
Wolfgang Amadeus Mozart

22

Sonata No. 14

K.457, 3rd Movement

Wolfgang Amadeus Mozart

(Die eingeklammerten Vortragsbezeichnungen gemäss den ältesten Ausgaben, das Autograph enthält, deren nur bei den Variationen des Themas und im Coda.)

[The performance indications in parentheses follow the earliest editions; the MS contains some only in the variations of the theme and in the coda.]

25

Sonata No. 18
K.570, 2nd Movement

Wolfgang Amadeus Mozart

Sonata No. 8, "Pathétique"
2nd Movement

Ludwig van Beethoven

Adagio cantabile.

Sonata No. 14, "Moonlight"
1st Movement

Ludwig van Beethoven

Für Elise

Ludwig van Beethoven

Nocturne
in G Minor, Op. 37, No. 1

Frédéric Chopin

Prelude
in E Minor, Op. 28, No. 4

Frédéric Chopin

Prelude
in C Minor, Op. 28, No. 20

Frédéric Chopin

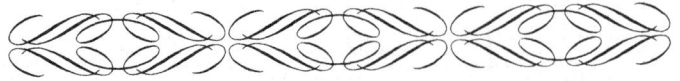

Consolation No. 3

Franz Liszt

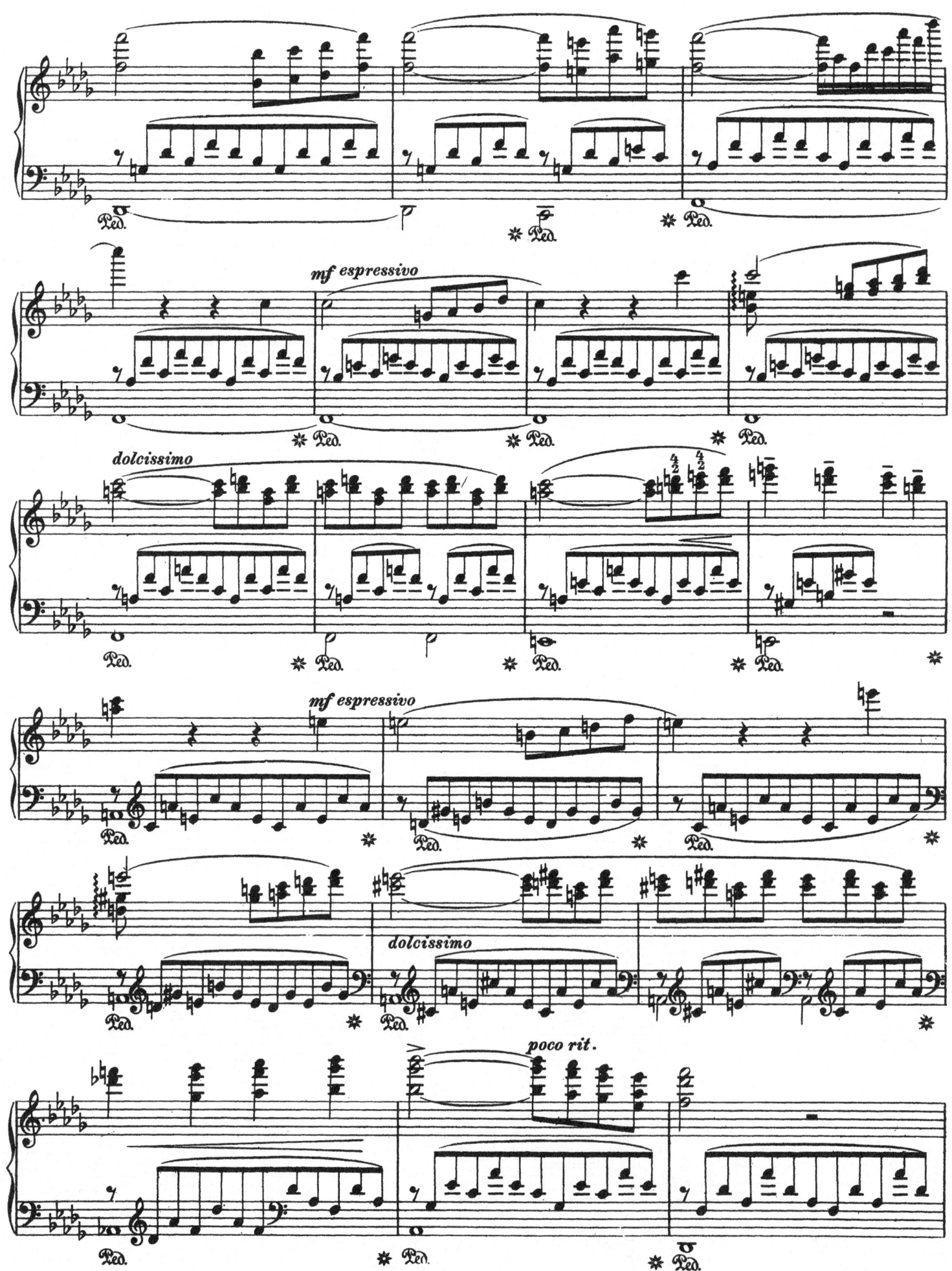

Consolation No. 4

Franz Liszt

Sonata in G Minor
Op. 105, 2nd Movement

Felix Mendelssohn

Adagio
from *Songs Without Words, Book II*, Op. 30, No. 3

Felix Mendelssohn

Adagio
from *Songs Without Words, Book IV*, Op. 53, No. 4

Felix Mendelssohn

Adagio
in E Major

Franz Schubert

Adagio
from *Adagio and Rondo*, Op. 145

Franz Schubert

Der Doppelgänger
(Originally for voice and piano)

Transcribed by Franz Liszt

Franz Schubert

65

66

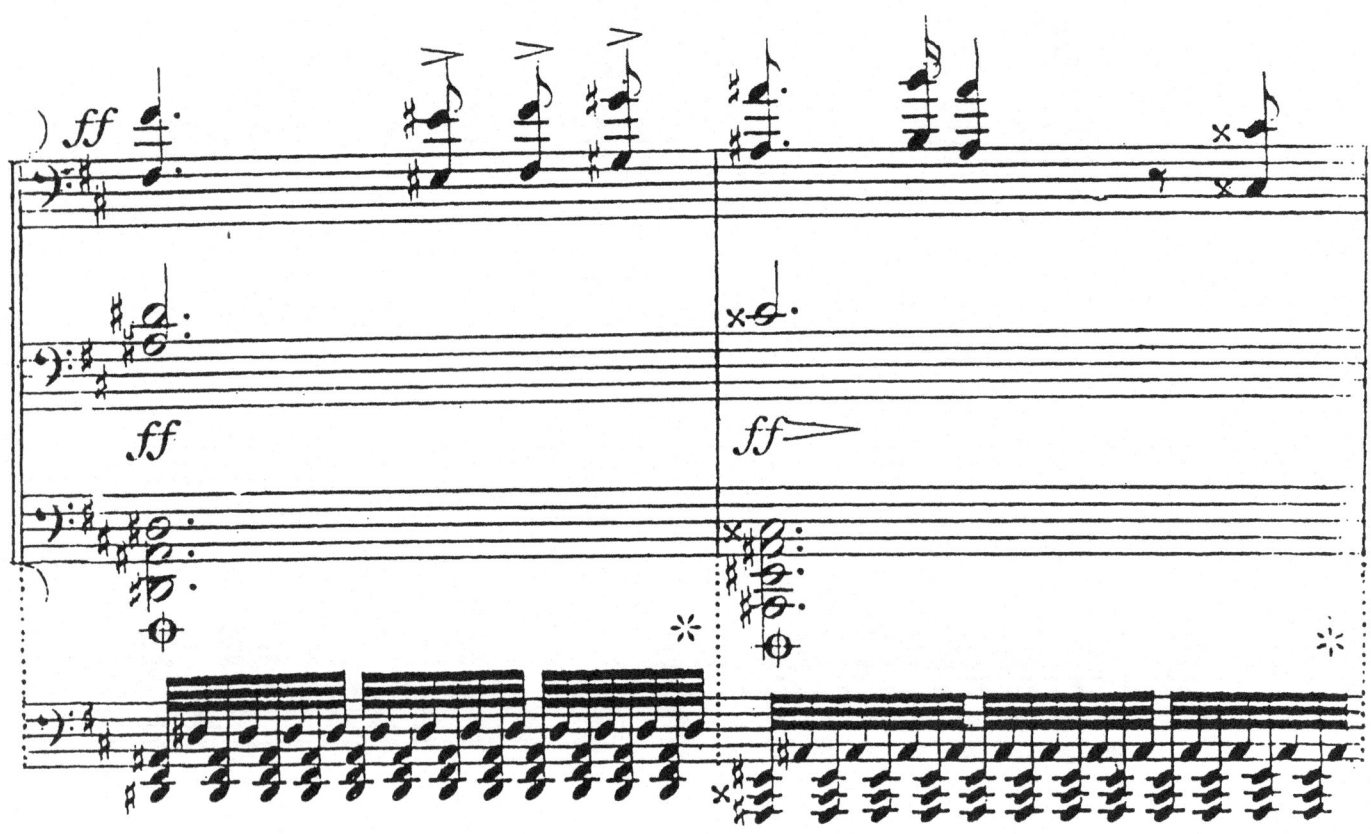

67

Traumerei
from *Kinderscenen*, Op. 15, No. 7

Robert Schumann

A Child Falling Asleep
(Kind im Einschlummern)
from *Kinderscenen*, Op. 15, No. 12

Robert Schumann

Warum?
[Why?]
from *Phantasiestucke*, Op. 12, No. 3

Robert Schumann

Eusebius
from *Carnaval*, Op. 9

Robert Schumann

Abendlied
from Op. 118, No. 3

Robert Schumann

Dedicated to her sister Marie Wieck

Larghetto
from *Four Fleeting Pieces*, Op. 15, No. 1

Clara Schumann

Intermezzo in E-flat Minor
from *Piano Pieces*, Op. 118, No. 6

Johannes Brahms

Nocturne No. 14

John Field

Nocturne No. 15
(Song Without Words)

John Field

On the Holy Mountain
[Na Svaté Hoře]
from *Poetic Tone Pictures,* Op. 85

Antonín Dvořak

In Tears
[V Pláči]
from *On the Overgrown Path, Book I*

Leoš Janáček

Larghetto.

Song of the Lark
from *The Seasons–March*, Op. 37b

Peter Ilyitch Tchaikovsky

The Sick Doll
from *Album for the Young*, Op. 39, No. 7

Peter Ilyitch Tchaikovsky

The Doll's Burial
from *Album for the Young*, Op. 39, No. 8

Peter Ilyitch Tchaikovsky

Morning Prayer
from *Album for the Young,* Op. 39, No. 1

Peter Ilyitch Tchaikovsky

To the Comtesse de Mercy Argenteau, née Princesse de Chimay

In the Convent
from *Petite Suite*, No. 1

Alexander Borodin

A Tear
[Slyoza]

Modest Moussorgsky

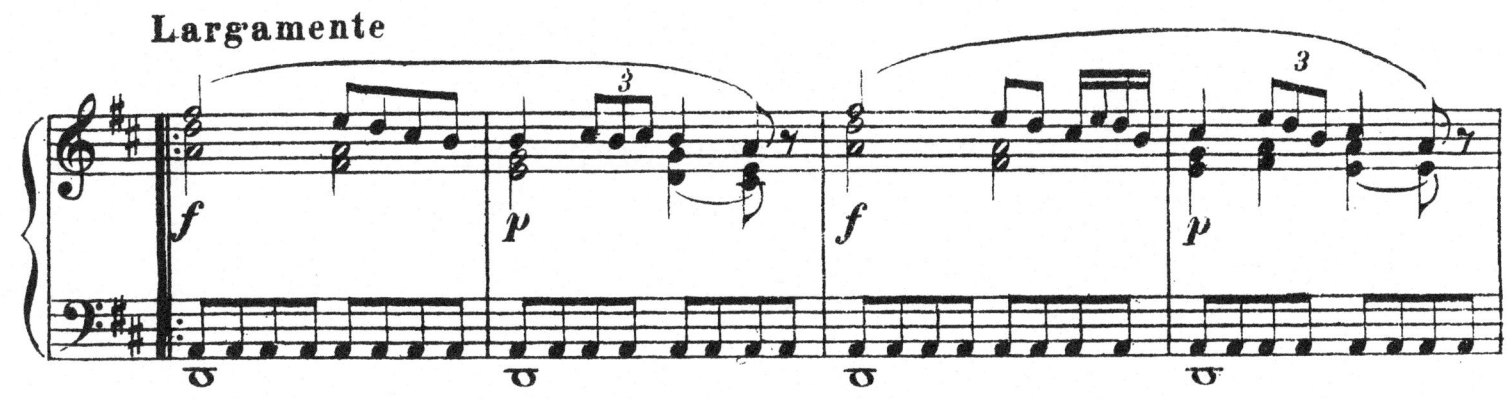

[1] In autograph no. 284 the upper part was originally written thus:

Catacombs–Roman Sepulchre
from *Pictures at an Exhibition*, Tableux 8

Modest Moussorgsky

*Before this section in the autograph there appears the following note by Moussorgsky (in Russian):

N.B.: Latin text: with the dead in a dead language. A Latin text would be suitable: the creative spirit of the late Hartmann [Gartman] leads me to skulls, summons me to them, the skulls have quietly lit up.

To Josef Silvinski

Prelude in A-flat Major
from *24 Preludes*, Op. 64, No. 17

César Cui

The Dying
from *The Months–November*, Op. 74

Charles-Valentin Alkan

Slow Dance
[Danse Lente]

César Franck

Élégie
from *Ten Characteristic Pieces*, Op. 10, No. 5

Jules Massanet

Lento, ma non troppo

Prelude
Op. 74, No. 4

Alexander Scriabin

Prelude
Op. 16, No. 4

Alexander Scriabin

The Swan
from *The Carnival of the Animals*

Camille Saint–Saëns

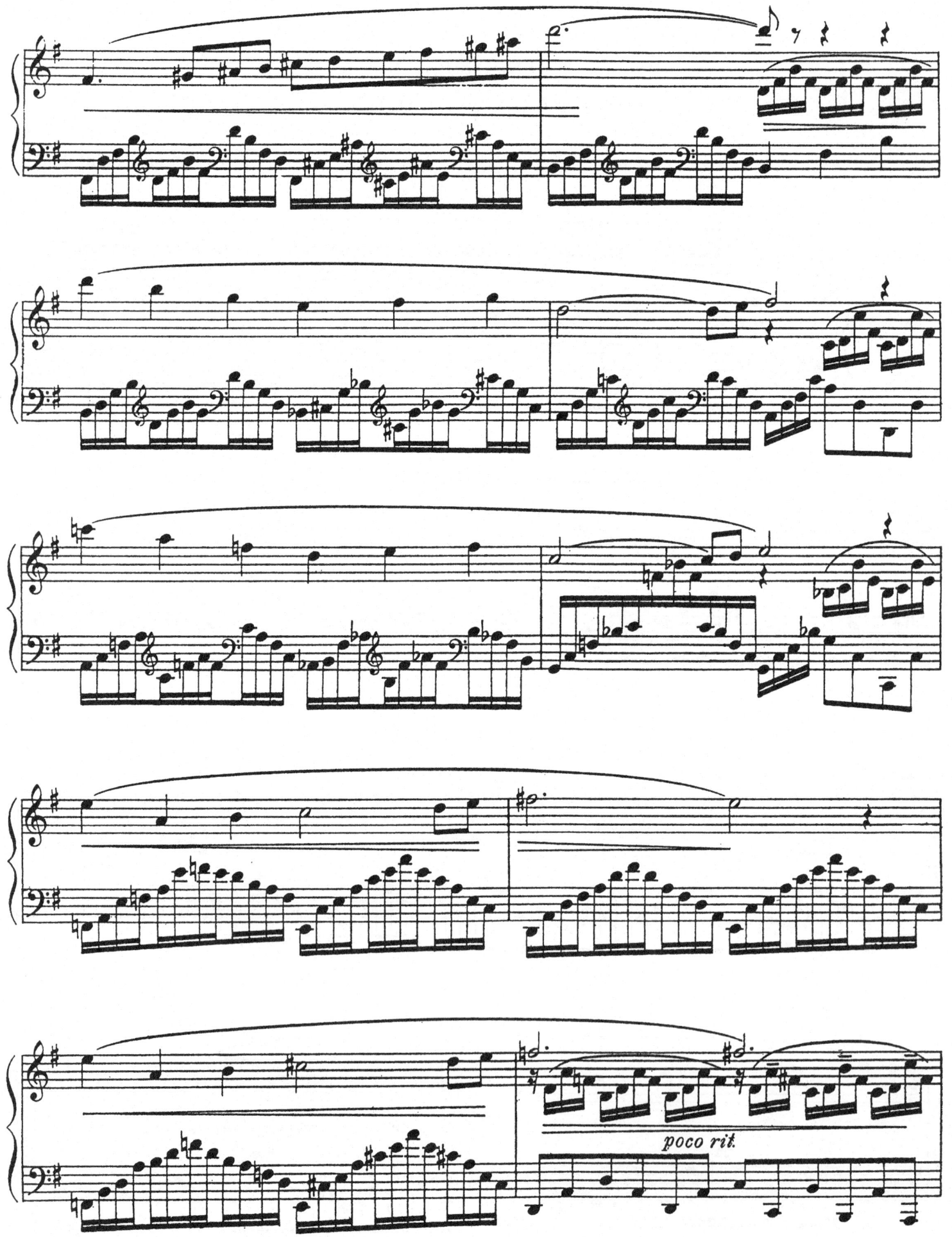

Elegy in G Minor
from *24 Characteristic Pieces*, Op. 36, No. 16

Anton Arensky

To A Wild Rose
from *Woodland Sketches*, Op. 51, No. 1

Edward MacDowell

A Deserted Farm
from *Woodland Sketches,* Op. 51, No. 8

Edward MacDowell

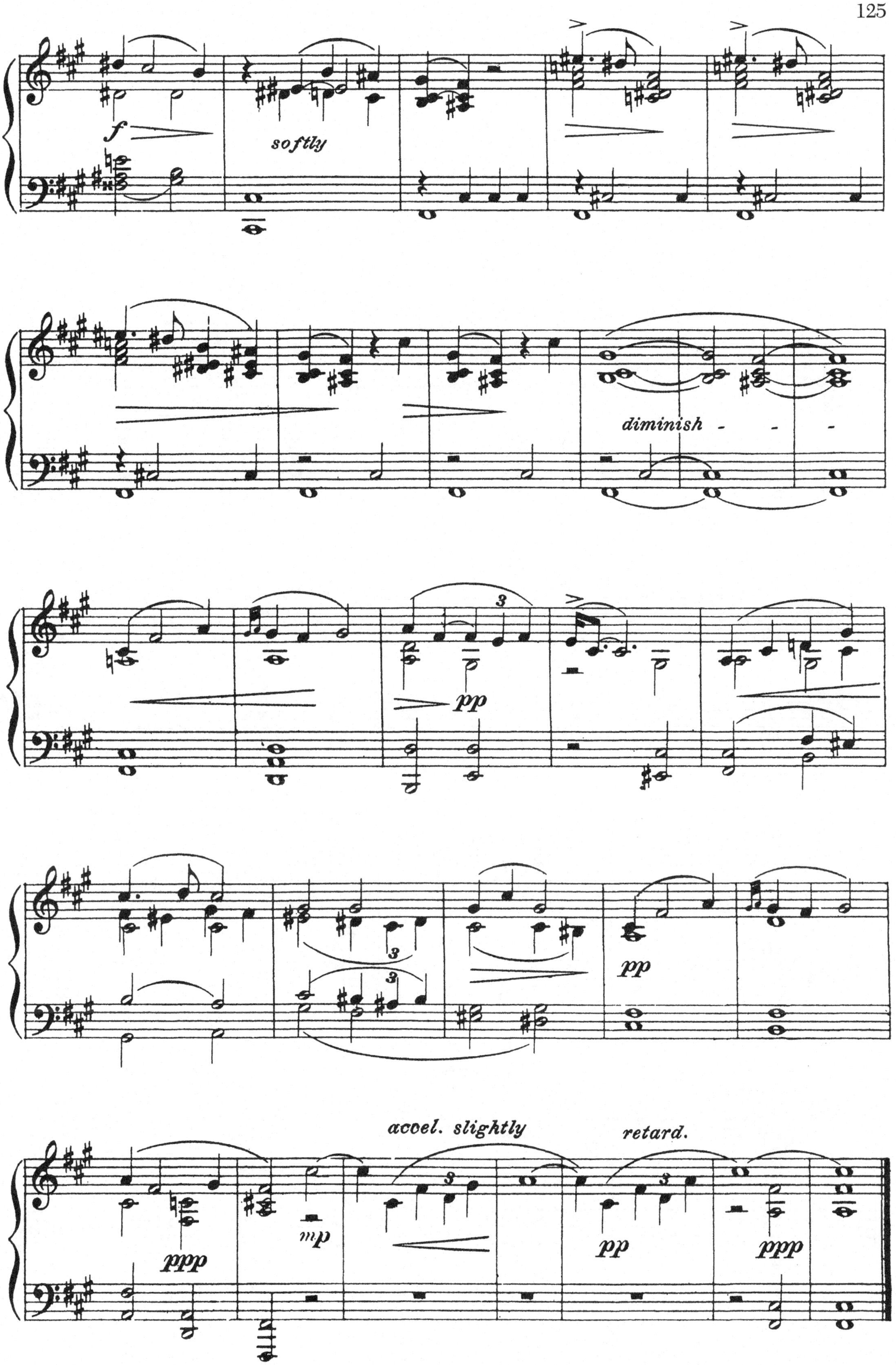
f
softly
diminish - - -
pp
pp
accel. slightly
retard.
ppp
mp
pp
ppp

Morning Mood
from *Peer Gynt*, Op. 23

Edvard Grieg

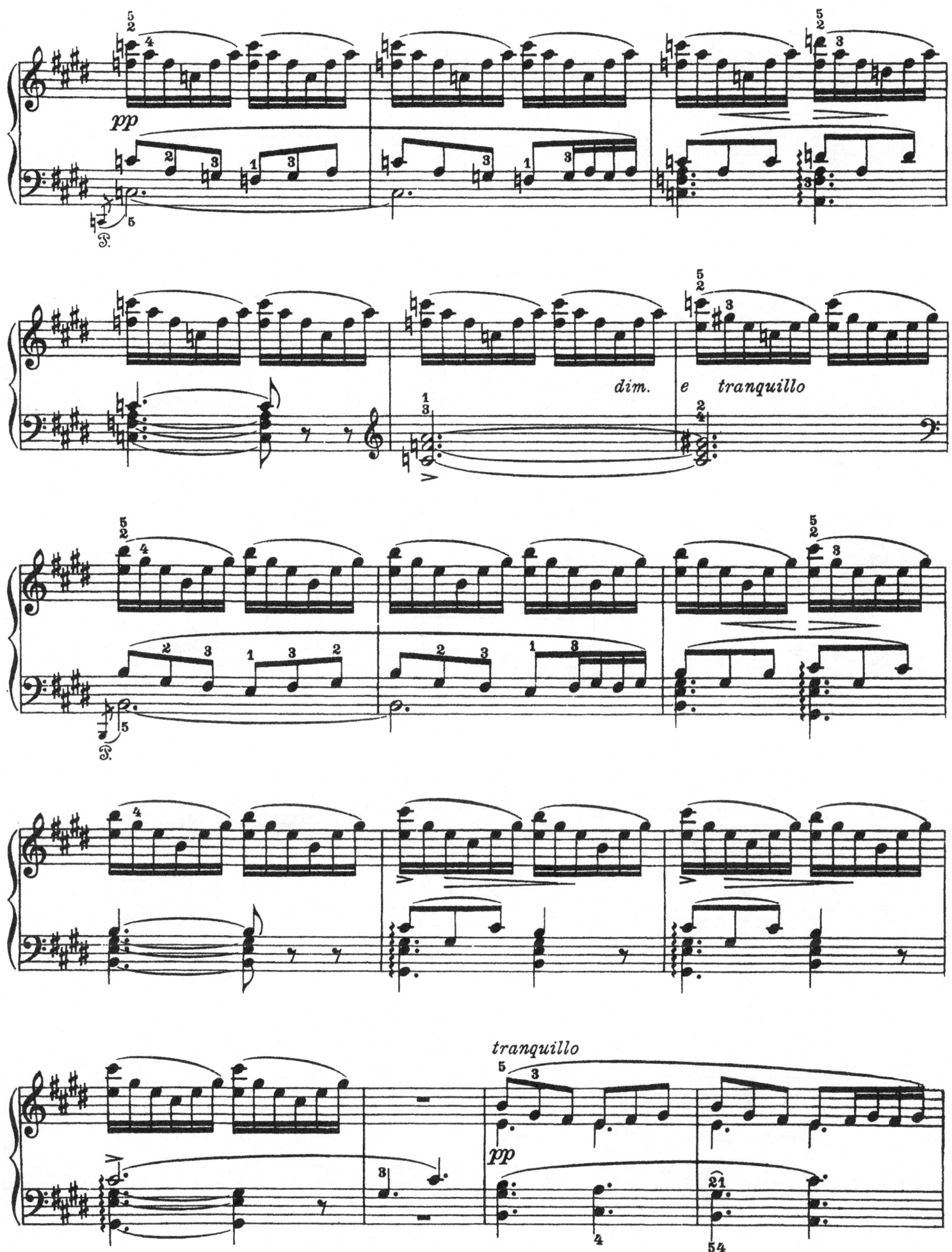

Girl with the Flaxen Hair
[La Fille Aux Cheveux de Lin]
from *Preludes, Book I*, No. 8

Claude Debussy

Claire de Lune
from *Suite Bergamasque*

Claude Debussy

134

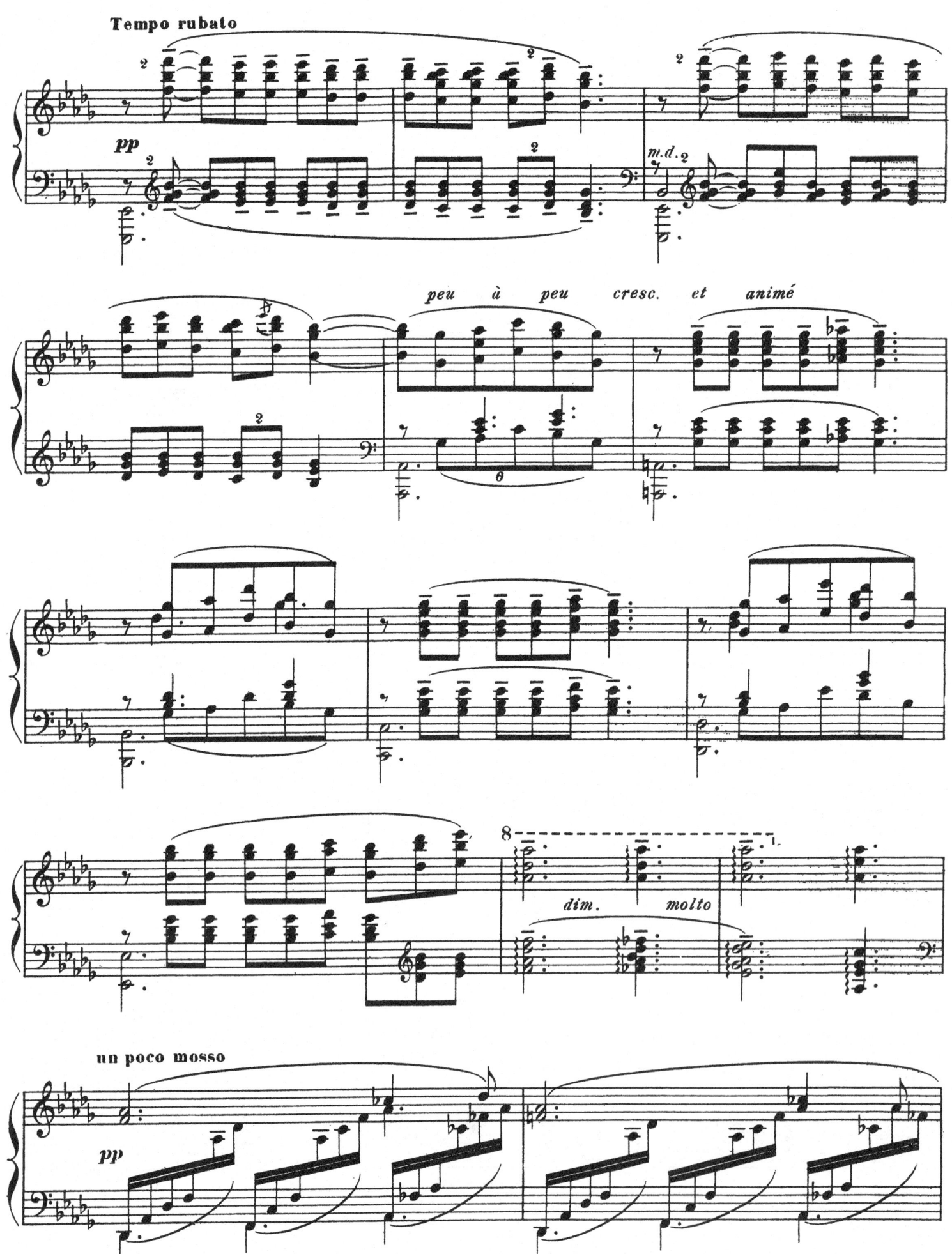

136

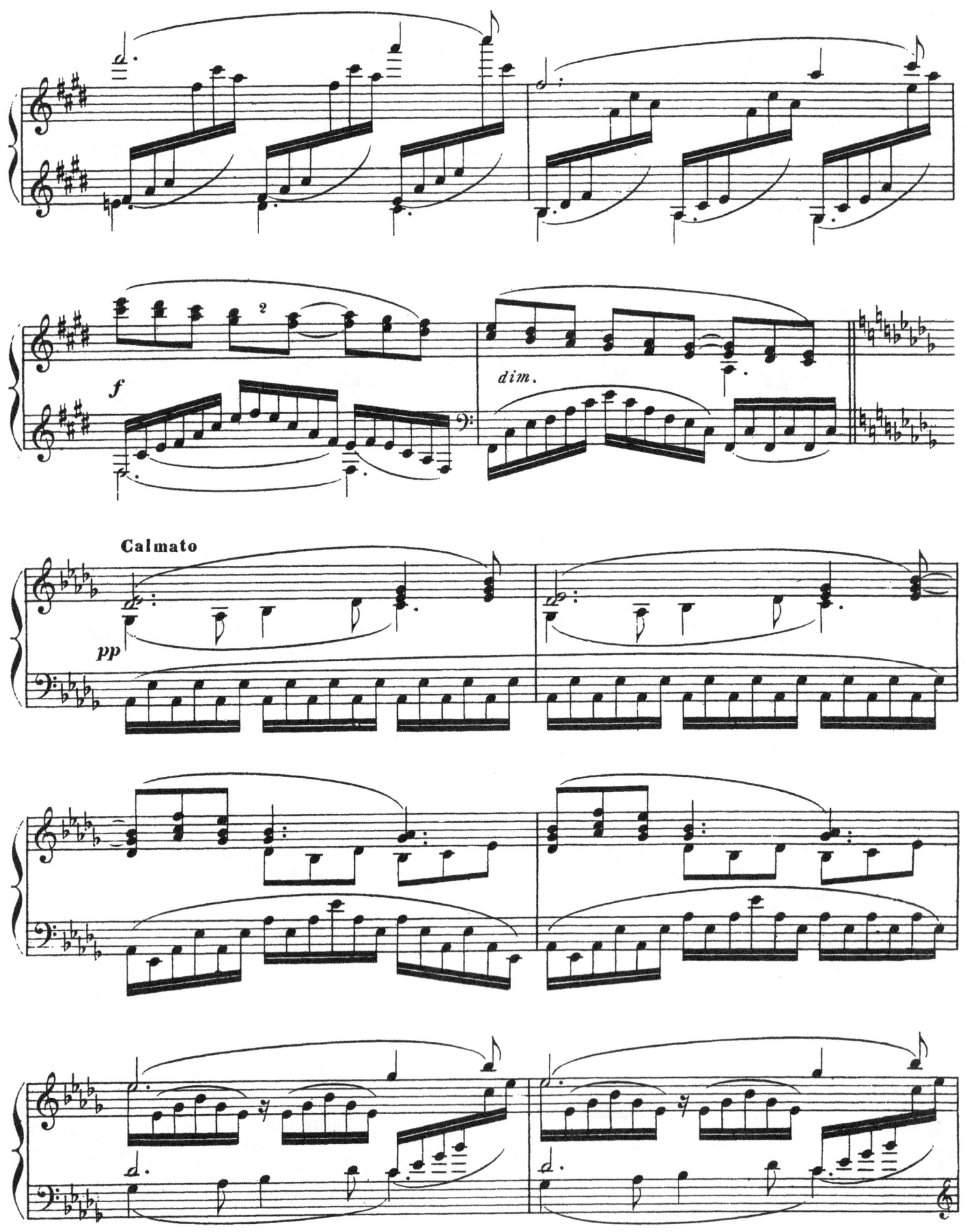

Jimbo's Lullaby
from *Children's Corner,* No.8

Claude Debussy

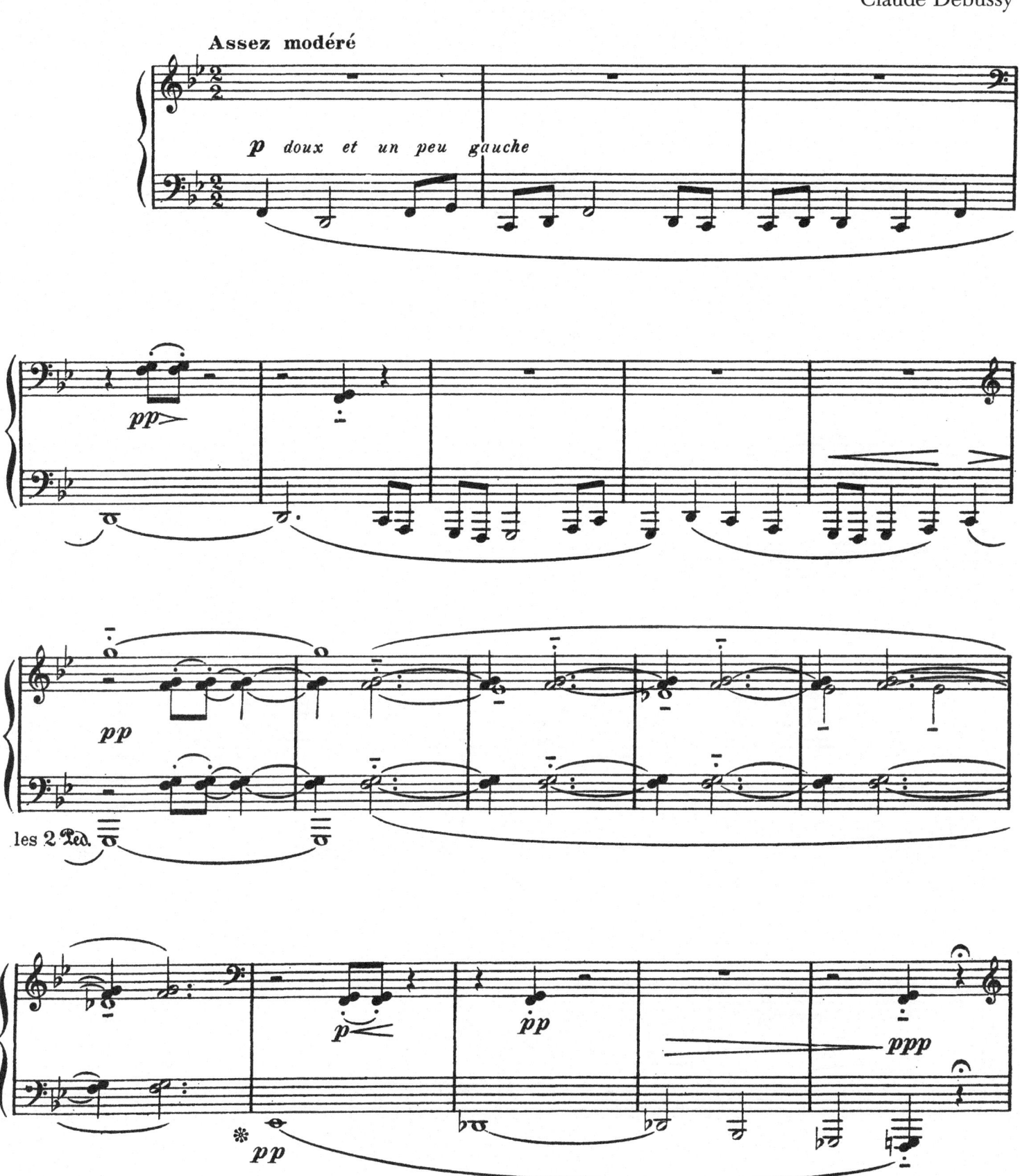

140

141